I am a penguin!

By Camilla de la Bedoyere

Miles Kelly

Look out for the 'Ask for help!' boxes. You will need help from an adult to do these activities.

Ask for help!

First published in 2014 by Miles Kelly Publishing Ltd
Harding's Barn, Bardfield End Green, Thaxted, Essex, CM6 3PX, UK
Copyright © Miles Kelly Publishing Ltd 2014

10 9 8 7 6 5 4 3 2 1

Publishing Director Belinda Gallagher
Creative Director Jo Cowan
Editorial Director Rosie Neave
Senior Editor Sarah Parkin
Designer Jo Cowan
Image Manager Liberty Newton
Production Manager Elizabeth Collins
Reprographics Stephan Davis, Jennifer Cozens, Thom Allaway, Anthony Cambray, Lorraine King

All rights reserved. No part of this publication may be reproduced, stored in a retrieval system, or transmitted by any means, electronic, mechanical, photocopying, recording or otherwise, without the prior permission of the copyright holder.

ISBN 978-1-78209-510-1

Printed in China

British Library Cataloguing-in-Publication Data
A catalogue record for this book is available from the British Library

Answers from pages 16–17

Lucky catch
Polly caught a fish

Odd one out
Duck

True or false?
1. True
2. False – they are called chicks
3. True

Who's who?
1. Chinstrap – B
2. Jackass – C
3. Macaroni – A

Find the penguin
JACKASS
GENTOO
EMPEROR

ACKNOWLEDGEMENTS

The publishers would like to thank Joe Jones and Richard Watson (Bright Agency) for the illustrations they contributed to this book.

All other artwork from the Miles Kelly Artwork Bank.

The publishers would like to thank the following sources for the use of their photographs:
t = top, b = bottom, l = left, r = right, c = centre,
bg = background, rt = repeated throughout

Cover (front) Gordon Court/ Hedgehog House/Minden Pictures/Corbis, (back, tr) aldorado/Shutterstock, (back, cl) Stubblefield Photography/Shutterstock
Ardea 15(t) D. Parer & E. Parer-Cook
Corbis 6 Tim Davis; 7(t) Frans Lanting, (b) Yva Momatiuk & John Eastcott/Minden Pictures; 10 Tim Davis; 11(t) Andy Rouse; 15(b) Michael S. Nolan/Robert Harding Specialist Stock; 20 Wayne Lynch/All Canada Photos; 21(b) Frans Lanting
Nature Picture Library 11(b) David Tipling;
Photo Discs/Digital Stock Heading bar (rt)
Shutterstock Joke panel (rt) Tropinina Olga; Learn a Word panel (rt) donatas1205; Learn a Word cartoon Nelia Sapronova; 1 niall dunne; 2 Palo_ok; 3 Moritz Buchty; 4–5 Eric Isselée; 5(bl) Jordan Tan, (r) Jan Martin Will; 8–9(bg) Lucy Baldwin; 8 & 9(heading bar & panel b) buruhtan; 8(penguin panel tr) Joney, (brush stroke tl) Ambient Ideas, (speech bubble br) tachyglossus; 9(panel tr) april70; 12–13 lfstewart; 13(tr) Karel Gallas; 14 Mogens Trolle; 16–17(bg) llaszlo; 16(heading bar) bruniewska, (panel tr) andrewshka, (penguins cl) Memo Angeles; 17(panel tl) donatas1205, (panel tr) pichayasri, (heading panel b) Veerachai Viteeman, (panel b) samiah samin, (brush stroke b) Ambient Ideas; 18 AndreAnita; 19(t) Anders Peter Photography, (b) steve estvanik; 21(t) Mogens Trolle

Stickers All Shutterstock (tr–bl) andere andrea petrlik, andere andrea petrlik, pichayasri, yorgos, Marc Sublet, Memo Angeles

Every effort has been made to acknowledge the source and copyright holder of each picture. Miles Kelly Publishing apologizes for any unintentional errors or omissions.

Made with paper from a sustainable forest

www.mileskelly.net
info@mileskelly.net

Use your stickers to illustrate the story.

And these are for fun!

Contents

What are you?

I am a penguin!

I am a bird, but I cannot fly. I spend most of my life in the sea.

Waterproof feathers

Humboldt penguin

Flippers

Webbed feet

Q. Why do penguins carry fish in their beaks?

A. Because they haven't got any pockets!

Strong beak

White chest

Penguin family

There are 17 types of penguin. These seabirds stand upright and have short legs.

Emperor penguin
115 centimetres tall

Little penguin
35 centimetres tall

How fast can you swim?

LEARN A WORD:

streamlined

A shape that is ideal for moving quickly through water or air.

I am a speedy swimmer!

My wings are more like flippers. They help me to 'fly' through the water. My body is streamlined.

King penguins

6

Walking on ice

Penguins waddle when they walk. Sometimes they slide on the snow and ice on their fronts.

Q. What goes black, white, black, white, black, white?

A. A penguin rolling down a hill!

Emperor penguins

Bouncy!

Rockhopper penguins hop from rock to rock by the sea.

Activity time

Get ready to make and do!

Penguin hunt

Look in books and on the Internet to try and find the names of all 17 types of penguin. Then look at pictures and draw your favourites.

Draw me!

YOU WILL NEED:
pencils · paper

1. Draw two squashed circles for the penguin's head and body.

2. Add the eye, beak, neck, flipper, tail and feet.

Now colour me in and give me a name!

3. Draw the penguin's chest. Now shape the tail and feet.

Ask for help!

Little friends

YOU WILL NEED:
coloured felt · scissors
toilet roll tube · glue
marker pens

HERE'S HOW:
1. Cut felt shapes for the penguin's eyes, beak, belly, flippers and feet.
2. Cover the toilet roll tube with black felt and glue it down.
3. Glue the felt pieces into place.
4. Draw on extra details, such as the eyes.

Penguin biscuits
YOU WILL NEED:
packet of plain, round biscuits
icing pens in different colours
or coloured royal icing

HERE'S HOW:
1. Use black icing to colour in the top of the biscuit. Allow to dry.
2. Fill in the rest of the biscuit with white icing. Allow to dry.
3. Use other colours to add eyes, a beak and feet to your biscuit.

Now make lots of penguins so you have a whole colony to play with!

What are your babies called?

My babies are called chicks.

The female lays one egg and we both look after it. We rest the egg on our feet so it does not get cold. Our chick is growing inside it.

King penguin parents

Egg

Fluffy feathers

Penguin chicks have thick, fluffy feathers called down. Down helps them to stay warm.

Q. What is a baby penguin's favourite game?

A. Slide and seek!

Chilly chicks

When it snows chicks can get chilly. They huddle together in groups for warmth.

Emperor penguin chicks

Where do you live?

Gentoo penguins

I live in cold places!

Most penguins live near the South Pole, where it is very cold. There are lots of fish in the sea, so it is a good place to live.

12

Warm water

Some penguins like to be warm. Jackass (African) penguins live on beaches around South Africa.

Q. What do you call a penguin in a desert?

A. Lost!

What do you eat?

I eat fish.

My chick is too young to swim, so I catch a fish and feed it to him.

Gentoo penguins

Catching fish

Penguins catch fish in their beaks, which have sharp edges and hooks on the end.

Galapagos penguins

Q. Where do penguins go swimming?
A. At the South Pool!

Spiky tongues

Penguins have little spikes on their tongues. The spikes grip onto wriggling fish to stop them escaping.

Puzzle time

Can you solve all the puzzles?

Lucky catch

Which lucky penguin caught a fish? Trace the lines with your finger to find out.

Pippa   **Percy**   **Polly**

true or false?

1. Penguins are birds.
2. Penguin babies are called kittens.
3. Thick, fluffy feathers are called down.

16

Find the penguin

Starting with the letter in the middle of the circles, follow the letters in the wheels to find the names of three penguins.

Odd one out

Only one of these birds can fly. Do you know which one?

Penguin

Ostrich

Emu

Duck

Kiwi

Who's who?

Use these clues to match each penguin to its name.

1. **Chinstrap penguins** have black stripes under their chins.

2. **Jackass penguins** have black and white faces.

3. **Macaroni penguins** have yellow crests.

Find the answers on page 2.

What do you look like?

I am colourful!

All penguins have black and white feathers, but some of us have yellow, red or orange feathers too. I have a yellow crest (head feathers).

Royal penguin

Q. What is black and white, and red all over?

A. A shy penguin!

Yellow eyes

Shy birds that live in New Zealand, yellow-eyed penguins are now very rare.

LEARN A WORD:

rare

When there are very few alive in the wild and they are uncommon.

Black faces

Adélie penguins have black faces. Males and females look the same.

Do you live together?

Yes, we live in big groups!

A group of penguins is called a colony. We make our nests in one place. Living together helps us to stay warm and safe.

Gentoo penguins

Show off!

Male penguins stretch up tall, point their beaks upwards, beat their flippers and call loudly to impress females.

Chinstrap penguin

Q. What is black and white and has eight wheels?
A. A penguin on roller skates!

Fight time

Penguins sometimes fight with each other. They call loudly and flap their flippers.

King penguins

21

Poppy goes on holiday

Use your stickers to illustrate the story.

Poppy the penguin didn't like snow. She lived near the South Pole in Antarctica, where there is snow everywhere.

One day, the other penguins gave Poppy a plane, a map and a mobile phone. They said she should go somewhere warm and have a holiday.

Poppy looked at the map and decided she would go to Africa. She said goodbye to her friends and flew off in her plane.

When Poppy got to Africa she went to the seaside and read her book in the sunshine. She ate lots of ice cream, but it didn't taste as nice as fish. Poppy sent a text to her friends: I am too hot and I don't like ice cream.

They replied: Go for a swim and find some fish to eat!

Poppy got back in her plane and flew to a river. She jumped into the water. It was lovely and cool, and there were lots of fish to eat.

But there was something else in the river too – a crocodile! *Snap, snap* went the crocodile's jaws as it chased Poppy. She jumped out of the river and took a photo of the crocodile with her

phone. She sent it to her friends with another message: I don't like crocodiles!

They replied: Go to the North Pole. There are no crocodiles there!

So Poppy flew her plane to the North Pole. She stepped out of the plane and dived into the icy water, where she found lots of fish.

She sent a text to her friends: This is just like home. I like it here!

And they replied: Watch out for polar bears!

Poppy looked around and saw a huge white bear running towards her. She jumped into her

plane and, as she flew back to the South Pole, Poppy thought that there is no place like home!

By Camilla de la Bedoyere